Bitch Slap APA

NATHANIEL SIMMONS, PH.D.
JOHN C. BYERLY

ISBN: 1517256607
ISBN-13: 978-1517256609

Library of Congress Control Number: 2016919637
CreateSpace Independent Publishing Platform, North Charleston, SC

Printed by CreateSpace, An Amazon.com Company.
Available on Kindle, Amazon.com, CreateSpace.com, and other retail outlets.

For further information on how you may Bitch Slap APA, please visit:

https://www.facebook.com/bslapAPA

DEDICATION

To those who have been bitch slapped by APA in the past, this book will help teach you how to bitch slap it back!

Oh, and to the anonymous student who said Dr. Simmons is "APA CRAZY…" You're right. In fact, he is so crazy about APA he co-authored this fucking book!

Eat it.

CONTENTS

ACKNOWLEDGMENTS

Thank you Professor Debbie Gamble for being such a hard ass on Nathaniel. He learned APA because of you…even though he slightly hated you for it at the time. ☺

Special thanks to Amanda Piering for helping Nathaniel with brainstorming this bad ass title and early conceptions of this book!

1

WTF IS APA

The American Psychological Association (APA) created a way to format our shit and get all of our ducks in a row when writing papers, essays, and research. They call this "APA format." Your professors and employers will refer to this as "APA." So, APA made APA for APA to confuse us all. Some conspirators may argue that APA made APA to fuck with us and see if we'd conform and do what they say. Well... it's working. The Social Sciences (i.e., Communication, Psychology, Sociology, etc.) use APA as their standard for formatting papers.

So, why do I need this shit, you ask? If you're a student, because your teacher, professor, college, or university said so. If that's the case, buck up and do your shit so that you can get the fuck outta Dodge! Everything has hoops. Life is one big fucking hoop. Your job will have hoops. Jump pony jump. But, don't just jump, show them that you can do fucking backflips like an Olympian.

If you're just another nerd like Dr. Simmons... well you need this to publish your research in certain journals (even though they might do an abridged APA). Further, if you like things to look pretty and enjoy being told what to do, then APA is for you! As one of our English professors would always say, (when speaking of MLA which is another beast that we won't even touch with a 20 foot pole in this book) "We need a common way to look up research." In other words, if you follow APA correctly, we will all understand how to locate the book, magazine, journal article, etc. and won't be wondering what the hell you are talking about and if we can even find whatever it is the fuck you were trying to write. It makes that shit nice and tidy! However, this doesn't mean APA is nice, or easy.

APA is a bitch, so you better bitch slap it before it bitch slaps you! Follow our instructions. We know our shit and will tell you what the fuck to do and how the hell to do it. So listen up! And fucking try, no one likes a bitch who doesn't try.

So, how the hell do I use this book? This book isn't necessarily meant to be read cover to cover. Instead, look up what shit you need and save yourself some fucking time.

Chapter Two covers the fucking fundamentals of APA. In chapter two, you will learn about basic shit such as levels of heading, what fucking font to use, and how the hell your paper should look in APA format. This is basic shit.

Chapter Three reviews titles pages and abstracts. In other words, in chapter three, you will learn how the hell your title page and abstract should look, as well as what the fuck to include within each.

Chapter Four shares APA mechanical bull shit and tells you the basic shit you need to know about punctuation, block quotes, parentheses, and capitalization, etc. It's annoying as well, but it's the way APA is, so follow our fucking advice.

Chapter Five tells you how the make the baddest bad ass reference list ever. We share what the fuck to include within your reference list and tips to guide your reference list construction.

Chapter Six covers in-text citations and related shit. Learn how to cite in-text one or multiple fucking authors. We even made you a fancy ass chart to make your shit easy, so fucking use it.

Chapter Seven perhaps lists more mother fucking APA examples than you might want. We offer reference examples for all sorts of shit like books, journals, and online magazine articles. We even include in-text citations for each mother fucking APA example we share.

Chapter Eight reveals how to annotate your references based off APA sensibilities. For whatever reason, APA doesn't share how the hell to make an annotated reference list, so we guide you on what an annotation could look like. APA isn't perfect, such as life.

Chapter Nine reviews 25 common fuck ups that are common within APA users. Here, you will learn ways to NOT fuck it up, as you work towards being a bitch slapping goddess. BAM!

Chapter Ten shares snapshots from a fucktastic sample paper Dr. Nathaniel Simmons wrote. Within those snapshots, you'll see visual examples of items discussed in this book such as levels of heading and reference lists.

2

FUCKING FUNDAMENTALS

Welcome to APA Fucking Fundamentals 101. In this chapter, we discuss what the fuck to do about your font, spacing, margins, and so forth. Wanna know how to make a list or levels of heading in APA? Then, this chapter is for you bitch. Lost already? No worries, cozy on up to APA like it is your next casual encounter and let's get this shit done.

Font
The APA font of choice is Times New Roman, 12 point font. We wrote this fucking book in Times New Roman to help you know what it looks like. Sometimes people might be down with Calibri, 11 point font because that is usually the default now in Microsoft Word, but whatever – stick with Times New Roman and don't be a whiny cunt. Just take the time to switch it.

Spacing
Double-space your shit! Yes, all of it! Enough said.

Margins
Margins should be one-inch all around. One fucking inch!

Active vs. Passive Voice
APA requires that you write in active voice, not passive. Your employer or professor may not give a shit, so ask them for a fucking preference if

you're that worried about it. Otherwise, avoid that shit like the plague.

Active: I conducted the study in Japan.
Passive: The study was conducted in Japan.

If you really struggle with this shit, your word processor probably is able to detect whether or not your sentence is active or passive. Look that shit up. For this book, we wrote however the fuck we wanted. Deal with it.

Lists (AKA Seriation)

Listing items out can help make shit clear and make your writing clear as fuck. In APA, you may use Arabic numbers (1, 2, 3, etc.), lowercase letters within parentheses, and bullet points for lists. Double-space your shit, because your whole document should be double-spaced. If you are writing or using lists of shit in your paper, here's what you should do.

If you want to use Arabic numerals, you should follow them with a period, as follows:

To make it fucktastic, we recommend:

1. Don't fuck it up.

2. Learn your shit.

3. Make it snazzy.

Bulleted lists may use circles, squares, and anything the fuck you want, as long as it isn't too crazy. In fact, using the example above, you could also make it fucking snazzy with bullet points, like so:

To make it fucktastic, we recommend:

- Don't fuck it up.

- Learn your shit.

- Make it snazzy.

You may also use lowercase letters within parentheses inside a sentence to list a series of items.

When doing APA format you might (a) fuck it up, (b) do it fucking right the first time, or (c) do it fucking right the second time.

Notice that you should use commas because there are no internal commas. If you have internal commas, use a semicolon between your lists.

When doing APA format individuals are rated as: (a) lower performers, who can't get it up; (b) high performers, who get it up; and (c) mediocre performers who only get it semi-up.

Headers
There are five possible formatting ways to organize your headers within your paper. Don't label your introduction. We fucking know that when you start your paper that it is your introduction. So, don't label that shit. Frankly, APA doesn't give a fuck about your introduction enough to label it!

Following this fucking format for your levels of your heading:

1. **Center that shit. Make it bold. Use Uppercase and Lowercase Headings (any word four letters or more should be capitalized).**
2. **Flush that shit left. Bold it. Use Uppercase and Lowercase Heading (any word four letters or more should be capitalized).**
3. **Indent that shit. Bold it. Lowercase that paragraph heading and end that shit with a period (only capitalize the first word dumbass).**
4. ***Ident that shit. Bold it. Italicize it. Lowercase that paragraph heading and end that shit with a period (only capitalize the first word dumbass).***
5. *Ident that shit. Italicize it. Lowercase that paragraph heading and end that shit with a period (only capitalize the first word dumbass).*

Below is an example of what headers might look like for a research project on pugs.

Note: We added the (1, 2, etc.) to demonstrate the level of heading for clarity. **Don't put the (1, 2, etc.) after your title dumbass, just do what it says.** That's not fucking APA, that's us helping you to fucking bitch slap the hell out of it!

Pugs (1)

Colors of Pugs (2)

    Fawn pugs. (3)

    Personalities of fawn pugs. (4)

    Fawn pugs are the shit. (5)

    Apricot pugs. (3)

Pug Health Issues (2)

3

TITLE PAGES & ABSTRACTS

Title pages and abstracts are two key components people fuck up (see Chapter 9 for more common fuck ups). This chapter will show you how to bitch slap title pages and related components, such as a Running head, and abstracts. Read this shit, or risk being bitch slapped.

Title Pages
Title pages should be double-spaced and have (a) a Running head, (b) page number, (c) title, (d) author name, and (e) institutional/professional affiliation such as university or company name. Title pages should have a Running head and page number at the top of your paper. Titles should be in upper and lowercase letters, centered, and not more than 12 words. See Chapter 10 for an example of a title page.

Running head
A "Running head" is at the very top of your page (usually within the headers) and includes (a) an abbreviation of your title in CAPS and (b) a page number. The abbreviated title cannot be more than 50 characters long, including spaces. The word "Running head:" only appears on the title page. Thereafter, the Running head only includes the abbreviated title and not the word "Running head." Why? Because that'd be fucking repetitive.

Original Title: Taking Advantage of Being Foreign: Gaijin Smashing for Privacy Management

Running head: GAIJIN SMASHING

Abstracts

An abstract is a brief synopsis, or summary, of your paper that is typically only one paragraph long. Basically, an abstract shares the highlights of your paper in a condensed format for easy skimming so that people know what the fuck your paper is about. If you're submitting your research to a journal, you will, more than likely, need to submit an abstract as well. Unless otherwise instructed, abstracts are usually 100-250 words, plus keywords. Most professors don't want a fucking abstract, so be sure to ask if you're reading this shit for school.

Fucking format for abstracts:
- Put your abstract on page two of your document, right after your fucking title page.
- Label your abstract, "Abstract." It's fucking genius, right?!
- Abstract should be written at the top of your paper in upper and lowercase letters. It should NOT be in all fucking CAPS. That's just stupid.
- Center the word "Abstract."
- Do NOT indent your abstract.
- Once you've finished your abstract, on a new line, indent and write *"Keywords:"* Then, list keywords or "search terms" you think are relevant to your essay. Write your keywords all in lowercase. Don't fuck it up. The title "Keywords" should be written in italics. Your actual keywords should not be in italics.

Abstract

Summary of your shit here. Make it concise and interesting. Overview of your findings to make us wanna read it. Be fucking coherent. What methods did you use? What implications exist for your study?

Keywords: bull shit, coherency, bitches

4

APA MECHANICAL BULL SHIT

APA requires that you do shit a certain way. Why? Because APA fucking says so! For whatever reason we bought into the social construction that they are the gods/goddesses of paper writing, so we do what they say, so we don't get burned as fuck. So, listen up and do what they want, so you don't get the shit zapped out of you by lightning or something crazy like that... or better yet, so you don't get bitch slapped to hell and back! From spacing to block quotes, this chapters helps you bitch slap all the mechanical BS.

Spacing

Youaresupposedtohavespacingdumbass. See how reading that sucks? That's because you need to follow the following rules:

Space once (one time fucker!) after:
- between words (Shouldn't that go without saying? WTF?!)
- periods within references (Note: the word "within");
- periods of people who go by initials instead of their real fucking name such as the cool ass bitch J. K. Rowling; and
- semicolons; colons: and commas,

There's always a silly fucking exception. When I say "silly," I mean "fucking ridiculous," and that it'll drive you crazy. Yep, that's right! Don't ever....EVER space between periods in abbreviations such as a.m., p.m., i.e., e.g., etc. Colons in ratios also don't get extra spaces. For example, you have a 1:1 chance of being bitch slapped if you fuck this up.

According to APA (2010), "Spacing twice after punctuation marks at the end of a sentence aids readers of draft manuscripts" (p. 88). So, do you think that might mean that you should space twice after periods? YES!!! This isn't a fucking text message bitches, this is some pristine academic bullshit! That means, you better place two goddamn spaces after periods when you end a sentence. DO IT OR EAT SHIT!

Period
Periods in APA are pretty fucking common sense. For example, the U.S. should have periods, as should a.m. or p.m. to indicate what time of fucking day it is. This is bull shit you learned in the second grade. You should also use periods for initials of one's name such as J. C. Byerly.

At the same time, when you should NOT use periods should also be fucking common sense. Do NOT use periods for abbreviations and acronyms such as APA, CDC, NIMH, etc. Also, do NOT use periods for state abbreviations (Who the fuck would do that anyway?!).

Comma
APA uses what fancy shit call the "oxford comma." In other words, APA says that when you list shit out and it has three or more items, you best put a fucking comma there. For example:

I like apples, bananas, and strawberries.
Simmons, Byerly, and Chen (2020) said…

Beyond that, follow basic grammatical rules for using a damn comma. Use the breath test, when in doubt. If you feel as if you should pause and take a breath while reading your sentence, then you probably need a comma.

Commas are also used to clarify the fucking date, as shown below:

September 12, 2016, is the day I am writing this sentence, but I also wrote this in September 2016.

Semicolon
Semicolons are used to fucking separate two independent clauses that don't have a fucking conjunction.

Readers of *Bitch Slap APA* will learn shit; those who don't read it won't.

Semicolons are also used to separate comma series bullshit that could otherwise be confusing.

(Simmons, 2012; Simmons & Byerly, 2016)

Colon
In addition to correct fucking grammar, use the cunty colon in ratios (i.e., 1:2), and in your reference list between locations and publishers (i.e., New York, NY: Wiley).

Dash
Don't - use - the - damn - dash - too - much. It weakens the fucking flow! Instead, damn dashes should be used as only a sudden fucking interruption.

These two assholes – one from the A list and one from the B list – were evaluated individually.

Quotation Marks
Besides being used for direct quotations, quotation marks have a fucking purpose in APA. Double quotation marks should be used to introduce ironic comments, slang, or coined expressions. Additionally, double quotation marks should be used to make article or chapter titles pop.

Simmons' (2012) article, "Tales of gaijin: Health privacy perspectives of foreign English teachers in Japan"

Double & Single Quotation Marks
Double quotation marks should be used to enclose your fucking direct quotes. Therefore, if you have a quote within a quote, use single ' ' inside the quotation marks.

Simmons and Byerly (2016) said, "If you don't do this fucking easy shit, you might be what we call a 'dumbass'" (p. 69).

Block Quotes
Block quotes are any fucking quote with 40 words or more. Block quotes do not use fucking quotation marks. However, you should use double quotation marks for any quoted materials within your block quote. So, in other fucking words, always use double quotation marks as your go to and if you already have that shit, then use single within. Since block quotes are also indented in your text (which should be used fucking sparingly, learn to fucking paraphrase!), that indentation acts as your double quote marks, which is why you don't fucking need them around the whole damn quote!

Simmons (2012) found the following:

> ALTs might also benefit by increasing their knowledge of their host country's conceptions of privacy in preparation for immigration. Providing intercultural training on both sides of this interpersonal, intercultural relationship will provide participants with tools and vital information as they navigate such interactions. (p. 33)

Notice that the period in a block quote is also at the end of the sentence instead of after the parentheses. Don't fuck this up and don't do this anywhere else!

Parentheses
Parentheses get a lot of fucking use in APA. Parentheses should be fucking used:

- within APA in-text citations as shown in Chapter 6
- to introduce fucking abbreviations and acronyms

  Assistant Language Teachers (ALTs) in Japan...
  The Center for Disease Control (CDC) is....

- When using letters to list a series of items

Fucking bullshit is composed of (a) one part bull, (b) one part shit, and (c) a lot of hot air.

Brackets

Depending upon your writing style and whatever the hell you are writing, you may or may not use brackets. However, brackets can be bad ass, especially if you want to add your own damn two cents. For example, you may use brackets to add your voice within a direct quotation.

"when [others'] bull shit is examined, it stinks" (Fake, 1950, p. 1).

Capitalization

Besides basic grammar shit, make sure that you capitalize:

Titles & Headings

Remember that there is a fucking difference in-text writing and reference writing. In your references, you would only capitalize the first word of a title and the first word of a subtitle. However, if you are saying, "In the book *Bitch Slap APA*, every word would need to be fucking capitalized. However, if you had a book title with lots of conjunctions, article adjectives, and all that shit, you would capitalize it as *The Bitch that Slapped APA for the Next Two Years*. For all of your research nerds, if you are referring to a section header in your paper such as "in the Data Collection section" – then, YES, you would fucking capitalize "Data" and "Collection."

Proper Nouns

Whether it is the name of your mom, your friend, your beloved (or hated) professor/boss, then yes, you should always fucking capitalize proper fucking nouns. Also, specifics should be capitalized and generalizations should not. For example, if you are talking about a specific communication course, such as Communication 101, then yes, that should be capitalized. However, if you are talking about a general communication course, then fuck no, don't capitalize that shit!

Nouns Followed by Numerals or Letters

This bull shit right here is one reason why we fucking wrote this book. There are always weird exceptions and instances in APA. Bitch slap that shit, so that it doesn't bitch slap you! Here's the fucking rule: You should capitalize nouns that are followed by numerals (AKA numbers) or letters that denote some type of specific bull shit series. Like so:

On Day 454 of the fucking Observation 2
As shown in Table 1, Figure 27B, and Chapter 1
Grant FU6969 from the National Institute of Fuck You.

Titles of Tests
If it is important enough to be a test, such as the Communication Apprehension Test, or the Ambivert Personality Test, then yes… do capitalize that fucker.

Italics
Generally, italics shouldn't be used that much. Yes, that's fucking vague. Thanks APA for that wise word of wisdom, assholes!

Here's what italics should be fucking used for:
- Titles (of books, periodicals, movies and such).
- Species, varieties, and genera of shit that you'll know if this makes fucking sense.
- When introducing a new term italicize it the first time only, but then stop. We don't wanna read a continually italicized word dammit.
- When using linguistic fucking examples
- Easily misread words
- Math shit such as letters as stats and variable crap
- Periodical volume numbers that should be in your fucking reference list.
- Scale descriptions such as 1 (*fucktastic*) and 5 (*fucking horrible*).

Don't fucking italicize the following:
- Chemical names like LSD and shit like that. H20? You know!
- Greek letters.
- Abbreviations (i.e., APA).
- Trigonometry terms such as tan, log, sin, etc.
- Foreign phrases

5

MAKING A BAD ASS REFERENCE LIST

APA calls a "bibliography" or "works cited" a "reference list," or "references" for short. The reference list should be double-spaced and should only include what you actually use, as a source, in your text. References should also have a hanging in-dent as demonstrated in Chapter 7. Remember to not include personal communications such as letters, emails, and interviews in your reference list. Instead, these should be cited in-text. Remember, reference lists exist to help people fucking find what you're citing, so it is important to have all of the reference components – which is exactly how this chapter will help you.

Reference Components
Generally, each reference should have an author, publication year, title, and publisher information. Publisher information might be the name of a formal publishing company like in a book, but it might also be a type of sponsoring organization like a newspaper name. As an author, it is your responsibility to make sure things are fucking right. Don't make us search because you fucked it up and left some shit out!

Authors
Authors' names should be written last name first and initials for first names. Take the fucking authors of this book for example (i.e., Nathaniel Simmons and John C. Byerly). We become Simmons, N., & Byerly, J. C. - it's that fucking simple. That's the rule for up to seven authors. If you have seven or more, list the first six fucking

authors' names, then put in three periods (AKA a mother-fucking ellipsis) and add the last author's name. Here are few more ways to bitch slap this APA shit:

- If you ever have authors who have the same last name, same first initial, but different first names, then you must list the first name in brackets.

Simmons, P. [Paul] (2015).
Simmons, P. [Phillip] (2015).

- If you have a fancy pants name with hyphens, keep the fucking hyphen! Do you want people to leave out shit from your name? No! You fucking don't. So, you keep the fucking hyphen and put a period after each initial as usual. So Yea-Wen Chen becomes Chen, Y.-W.
- Commas should be used to separate authors, including their names and initials. For two to seven authors, don't forget to also use the fucking ampersand (&) before your last author in your reference list.
- Group author names should be fully spelled out.
- If there's some punk ass author that wrote "with" some other bitch, the "some other bitch" gets the parentheses treatment. For example, is there was a book authored by Simmons, N. (with Byerly, J. C.) that is how it should appear in your reference list. For an in-text citation, only Simmons would get credit.
- If there is no author, the title moves to the author position, followed by the damned publication date.

Editors

Sometimes books have editors. Editors are bastards that get all of the money for the book, while individual chapter authors get a line on their resume that they wrote some shit. Editors do also add a fucking coherent voice and oversee the quality of the pieces, but yes…they get the fucking money in the end. Chapter authors don't get shit.

- When a book is "edited by," they are the main author, so they are the ones listed for the book. So, the editor's take the author slot and then add an (Ed.) or (Eds.) after the name to show "editor" or "editors."
- If you are citing a chapter in a book see Chapter 7 for additional examples, but in short it should appear as follows:
  Author last name, A. B. (2016). Title of fucking chapter. In A. B.

  Editor (Ed.), *Title of fucking book* (pp. xx-xxx). Location: Publisher

Date of Publication (AKA Publication Date)

- Generally, put the year inside parentheses after the author slot. It's that fucking simple.
- Magazines, newsletters, and newspapers are a bit different. In that case, put the fucking year and the exact fucking date in parentheses (month or month and day, year). If some dip shit lists it as a season, then put (season, year). Who the fuck dates things by seasons anymore besides on old family photographs?
- Fucking research papers and posters presented at academic bull shit conferences should give the year and month of the meeting (2016, November).
- If something has been accepted for publication, but they are moving as slow as fucking molasses on a cold winter's night, then list (in press) in parentheses, just like that as the year.
- Sometimes there is no fucking date and in that case use: (n.d.). That means no fucking date! But do some work, make sure there really is no fucking date before you just claim there's no fucking date. If it's a web page, look at the fucking entire page. It might be hiding at the fucking bottom!

Title

How you list a damn title, will depend on what type of fucking source it is, as follows:

- **Article and Chapter Titles:** Capitalize the first word of the title and subtitle only. Exception: Capitalize proper nouns.

  Cultural premises of privacy: Interrogating globalized workplace relationships in Japan.

- **Periodical titles:** For journals, newsletters, magazines and such, use upper and lowercase letters just like the fucking source does, but in italics.

  Journal of Bitch Slap

- **Non-periodicals:** For books and reports, capitalize the first word of the title and subtitle only. Of course if there is a proper noun, make sure that you capitalize it. (i.e., Japan). If you have an edition, report number, or volume number, place these in parentheses immediately after the title. However, don't put a period between the title and this information.

Developing bad ass APA habits (Publication No. FU-SOB-69-22).

Publication Information

In order to have a bad ass reference list, you have to do some homework, which often requires digging. References can make our life hell. Sometimes they don't always put everything we need on the same damn page, or easily viewable. So, it is up to us to do some fucking digging and find the information.

- **Periodicals:** Don't list periodical publisher names and locations. That's for books. No one gives a fuck about periodical shit like that. List the volume number after the fucking work's title. Italicize that shit. Only list the issue number in parentheses after the volume number if the journal is paginated separately by issue (i.e., each issue starts with page 1).

Bitch Slap Quarterly, 27, 443-456.
Journal of Bitch Slap, 26(3), 1-10.

- **Non-Periodicals:** Always list the fucking location (i.e., city and state if in USA, if outside of USA, also list city and country). Be sure to abbreviate state names and use a colon to split that shit up.

New York, NY: McGraw-Hill.
Akita, Japan: Akita International University Press.

Alphabetize your references

- Put references in ABC (just like a fucking dictionary tool) order according to the author's last name.
- Alphabetize by each letter. In cases where you have authors with the last name of "Black" and "Blacksmith," "Black goes first.
- Alphabetize chronologically. (e.g., Simmons, N., II. Precedes Simmons, N., III).

Work order

You know now to follow ABC order in your reference list. But WTF happens when you have some rock star publishing multiple pieces?

- Same-authored works are ordered by the year of publication with the earliest fucker first:

  Simmons, N. (2012).
  Simmons, N. (2013).

- Single, or one-author, work precedes multi-authored work. Even if the multi-authored work was published earlier, APA doesn't give a shit and neither should you!

  Simmons, N. (2012)
  Simmons, N. & Byerly, J. C. (2000).

- Multi-authored work that has similar, but different authors is arranged in ABC order by the first author, second, and so forth:

  Simmons, N., Apples, J., & Byerly, J. C. (2015).
  Simmons, N., Byerly, J. C., & Apples, J. (2016).

- Works with the same authors are arranged by publication year.

  Simmons, N. & Byerly, J. C. (2000).
  Simmons, N. & Byerly, J. C. (2005).

- Works with the same authors and same years need a lowercase "a, b, c" and so on immediately after the year inside the parentheses to make that shit clear on what is what.

  Simmons, N. & Byerly, J. C. (2000a).
  Simmons, N. & Byerly, J. C. (2000b).

- Works where authors have the same last name, but different first names are alphabetized by the first name initials:

  Simmons, A. & Byerly, J. C. (2005).
  Simmons, N. & Byerly, J. C. (2001).

- Works authored by groups are alphabetized by the first significant word/name of the organization. In other words dumbass, "the" or "a/an" doesn't fucking count! We are talking about groups such as the American Psychological Association and the National Communication Association. If there is no author, then the title should move to the author position and the same rules as above apply (i.e., alphabetize by the first significant word/name, etc.).

WTF is a DOI?

A DOI stands for "digital object identifier." It is essentially a way to find electronically-stored shit. Think of it as the fucking social security number for journal articles. You'll use DOI numbers for citing journal articles. Use this fucking format for DOI numbers in reference:

doi:xxx

Notice that there is no fucking space between the colon and number. Don't fucking flip out if the DOI is hellishly long. They do that shit to piss you off.

If there is no DOI for a journal (and there should be if it was published from 2000 to present), use the journal's home page in the following fucking format:

Retrieved from http://www.journalhomepage.com

Some dumbass bitches who don't know APA (I'm talking to you professors!), will ask you to provide the direct link to the article. We say do it the APA way, but we also aren't grading your shit… If you are graded incorrectly on this, you could always throw a bitch fit like you do about everything else and take your APA manual in and say, "BAM, I am right, you are wrong asshole!"

Disclaimer: We are not responsible for what happens after you act this way.

6

IN-TEXT CITATIONS & SHIT

Before you even start to worry or freak the fuck out about in-text citations and related shit, you best get yo' busted ass references together. You heard me. Return to this chapter once you have your mother fucking APA reference list legit! Make it right. Don't fuck it up! There's a reason for this, if you don't know what is in the asshole author location or year, then you can't properly do your in-text shit. Proceed, once you have your reference list together – you've been warned. Only then, will this chapter help you know how to make your in-text citations.

Reminder: Everything must be cited in-text with a corresponding reference EXCEPT some "holy" books and personal communications (see Chapter 7 for more).

APA Hack: Remember Author last name and year, and you should be set, but check out the following fucking formats on how to do particulars. Leave out all that Junior (Jr.) and Ph.D. bull shit. No one gives a fuck…well at least APA doesn't! Also, do your child a favor and don't make them a fucking junior. For realz. That ain't right.

Work by One Fucking Author
Using the author and date citation shit, here's what you do in-text, depending upon whatever style of writing you want:

Simmons (2012) found health privacy is important to foreign English teachers in Japan.

Do the above if you want to write a fucking narrative or some poetic Shakespeare bullshit. If you're less stylistically inclined, the following works too!

Health privacy is important to foreign English teachers in Japan (Simmons, 2012).

Note that the fucking author's last name only and the year of the publication (AKA the copyright) is what's listed. Don't forget that fucking comma! Notice also that the period is AFTER the citation. This isn't a direct quote. This is a mother fucking paraphrase! Don't you dare fuck this up, we're showing you what's what.

You could also write it like this which is known as a non-parenthetical citation (AKA no parentheses dumbass):

In 2012, Simmons' study of foreign English teacher privacy found...

Let's say you are writing a paragraph or long blurb about this one particular study. Well, in that case, you don't need to include the year in non-parenthetical citations after you do it the first time. However, if this shit can be easily confused with another, do have the year in addition to the author name.

Work by Multiple Fucking Authors
So, here's the deal. Depending upon how many authors you have, will depend on how you should bitch slap your APA.

If you have two authors, you must write those two bastards names all the time.

Simmons and Byerly (2016) explained
(Simmons & Byerly, 2016).

If you have three to five authors, then you have to list each of those assholes the first time you cite them, but after that you may use "et al."

First time usage:
Simmons, Byerly, and Brown (2007) uncovered...

Subsequent usages:

Simmons et al. (2007) uncovered...

Note the fucking exception: If the multiple authors names are very similar to another course such as "Simmons, Byerly, Heiner, and Brown (2007)" and "Simmons, Byerly, Smith, and Thompson (2007), then it would be important to list as many of the author names as possible to distinguish these sources. For example:

Simmons, Byerly, Heiner et al. (2007) and Simmons, Byerly Smith et al. (2007)

If you have six or more authors, then you get a break and may cite only the last name of the first author with et al. after it. Don't forget the fucking year! Be sure that, like detailed above, if you have works that have similar, but different author names that you list as much as possible to help keep these two straight. Table 6.1 will show you some mother fucking examples of this shit.

Group Authors

Groups can be fucking authors too! Usually these names are spelled out each time you fucking use them. Group authors might be corporations, associations, governmental organizations/agencies, etc. If something has a long ass name, you can shorten that bitch as long as you indicate so in-text. In other words, don't make up shit and expect us to all know what the fuck is going on in yo' head. There's some crazy shit up there and who are we to decipher? Here's what we mean:

The Center for Disease Control (CDC, 2016) explained.... Further, the CDC (2015) said...

If you want to abbreviate a very long name and not use an acronym, the general rule for APA is to make sure that you share enough information for it to be easily recognizable in the reference list. Related, if it's a long-ass name, you may abbreviate the name in the following citations and shit. Personally, just use an acronym, it is way less work, unless you are trying to write super long just to make a word count, you lazy bastard. See Table 6.1 at the end of this chapter for a visual.

Authors with the same fucking name

Due to uncreative parents, we have a bunch of bastards with the same damn name. These bastards grow up and publish work and make our life hectic. So, listen the fuck up on how to overcome this confusion and bitch slap authors with the same fucking name.

Sometimes authors have the same last name, but different first names. In that case, list their first initials in-text to help avoid confusion. This is particularly important if they have the same year. If they have different years, then logical people will fucking understand it could be someone different whenever they look at your reference list. For example:

Throughout research, N. Simmons (2014) and P. Simmons (2014) discovered…

Authors with the same fucking name and year

Shit can get confusing in APA, so to bitch slap it back into submission, make sure that if you have work by the same author and same year that you use a lower-case (a,b,c, etc.) to keep shit straight. Put this right after the year (i.e., 1983a). Do this in your reference list, but also in your in-text citation so that way they know which Simmons 2015a or Simmons 2015b to go to.

Research by communication scholar Simmons (2015a) said…
Further Simmons (2015b) found…

Work with no author, or anonymous

Occasionally, some work doesn't have an author or is written anonymously. Therefore, the title should be in double quotation marks (No title? Then look for a chapter or web page name). If you're writing the name of a periodical, book, or brochure, etc., be sure to italicize it.

("Title Example," 2010).
The book *Bitch Slap Your Mom* (2005)

If it is "Anonymous," then do the following:

(Anonymous, 2018).

Be sure that you alphabetize that shit accordingly in your reference list. "A" comes first dumbass!

Two+ works in the same parentheses

Sometimes you have to cite multiple works to make a point. For example, if you are doing a literature review and making a claim about a particular set of literature, then you need to cite how you've summarized that work together. When doing so, make sure that you put your citations in ABC order. In other words, they should follow your fucking beautiful alphabetizing skills that you demonstrated in your reference list.

(Byerly & Simmons, 2005, 2010).

What about in press shit, you ask? That goes last.

(Byerly & Simmons, 2005, 2010, in press).

What if you are making a point with different authors' works, like mentioned above? Alphabetize that shit within the parentheses.

(Byerly & Simmons, 2005; Simmons & Byerly, 2001).

Secondary sources (AKA a source within a source)

Secondary sources, or a source within a fucking source, should be used sparingly and almost never. However, dependent upon where you are in life, might influence how you proceed. For example, if you're an undergraduate student and your professor doesn't give a shit about secondary sources, then this is how you should do it. If you're a graduate student, you really need to go to the fucking original source. At the same time, sometimes documents are old as fuck and no longer accessible, so, in that case, a secondary source should be cited. Use your discretion, based upon your expectations (i.e., making your professor/boss happy, etc.). Be sure that you list in your reference list what you actually looked at. In most cases, you probably didn't go to the original if you are reading this, so, only list what you did use in your reference list. In-text, use the following:

Byerly said (as cited in Simmons, 2015)…

Citing specific parts of a work (like a page or chapter)

Sometimes you gotta cite specific shit. For example, if you're using a *direct quote*, you gotta tell them where the fuck you got it. That means providing the fucking page or chapter number. For example:

(Simmons, 2012, p. 15).
(Simmons & Byerly, 2016, Chapter 2).

Note that page is abbreviated as p. Chapter is not abbreviated. There's also a period after the parentheses.

Personal Communication(s)
Personal communication is anything that is fucking personal. This might be a letter, email, social media message, interview, telephone conversation, Tinder message, something your last hookup said to you, etc. In short, this should be data that isn't recoverable, per say. These are NOT included in the reference list, so don't fuck it up. To in-text cite this shit, give the first name(s) initials and the last name, personal communication, and exact date (or as exact as possible).

J. C. Byerly (personal communication, September 6, 2016)
(J. C. Byerly, personal communication, September 6, 2016).

Table 6.1. Basic Fucking In-text Citations

Type of Citation	First citation in-text	Subsequent in-text citations	Fucking Format	Fucking Format for subsequent in-text citations
Work by 1 Fucking Author	Simmons (2016)	Simmons (2016)	(Simmons, 2016).	(Simmons, 2016).
Work by 2 Fucking Authors	Simmons and Byerly (2016)	Simmons and Byerly (2016)	(Simmons & Byerly, 2016).	(Simmons & Byerly, 2016).
Work by 3 Fucking Authors	Chen, Simmons, and Kang (2015)	Chen et al. (2015)	(Chen, Simmons, & Kang 2015).	(Chen et al., 2015).
Work by 4 Fucking Authors	Byerly, Simmons, Brown, and Baker (2017)	Byerly et al. (2017)	(Byerly, Simmons, Brown, & Baker 2017).	(Byerly et al., 2017).
Work by 5 Fucking Authors	Beck, Aubuchon, Simmons, Tenzek, and Ruhl (2015)	Beck et al. (2015)	(Beck, Aubuchon, Simmons, Tenzek, & Ruhl 2015).	(Beck et al., 2015).
Work by 6+ Fucking Authors	Byerly et al. (2011)	Byerly et al. (2011)	(Byerly et al., 2011).	(Byerly et al., 2011).
Group Authors, with abbreviation	Center for Disease Control (CDC, 2015)	CDC (2015)	(Center for Disease Control [CDC], 2015).	(CDC, 2015).
Group Authors, no abbreviation	Bitch Slap University (2017)	Bitch Slap University (2017)	(Bitch Slap University, 2017).	(Bitch Slap University, 2017).

7

MOTHER FUCKING APA EXAMPLES

This chapter will contain the best mother fucking examples you've ever seen. Bluntly, your life will be fucking changed as you learn how to make a kick ass APA reference that's almost as perfect as Jesus! Read carefully and pay god damn good attention, don't mess this shit up. It's so easy, even a broke ass bitch could do it.

Follow the fucking format below. Look for the relevant information and plug it in. This shit is that easy.

You might be asking, can't I just use an online system to cite? Fuck no! They NEVER EVER, NEVER EVER WORK!! Do they work?! NO, they fucking don't!! Don't even think about trying that shit! It's a gateway drug to fucking up!

*Disclaimer: Not all the examples are legit research articles, books, and shit like that. We made some of this shit up because we got tired of spending too damn long looking for fucking legit items that were interesting. Deal w/ it. See, we are so tired after all this we can't even write "with!"

Index for Mother Fucking APA Examples

33. Online discussion groups
34. Electronic mailing lists
35. Blog Post
36. Blog Post Comment
37. Vlogs
38. Wikis
39. YouTube videos

Technical & Research Reports
40. Corporate authored government report
41. Corporate authored online task force report
42. Authored report from nongovernmental organization
43. Issue brief

Meetings & Symposium
44. Symposium contribution
45. Conference paper
46. Conference paper abstract
47. Invited lectures or workshops

Doctoral Dissertations & Master's Theses
48. Master's thesis
49. Doctoral dissertation

Audiovisual Media
50. Episode from a television series
51. Video
52. Podcast
53. Music recording
54. Map from the internet
55. Photographs

Court Decisions
56. Case

Legislative Materials
57. Federal testimony
58. Full federal hearing

Books, Book Chapters, & Reference Books

Fucking Format: The author's last name is written out and the first name(s) are abbreviated. Only one first name? Hellz yeah! The author saved you some time by not listing that shit. Add the title of the book, where it was published, and who published it.

Author, A. B. (year). *Title of work.* Location: Publisher
Author, A. B. (year). *Title of work.* doi:

Author, A. B. (year). *Title of work.* Retrieved from

   http://www.putyourwebsiteherebitch.com

Editor, A. B. (Ed.). (year). *Title of work.* Location: Publisher

1. Book, print version

Example:
Visage, M. (2015). *The diva rules: Ditch the drama, find your*

   strength, and sparkle your way to the top. San Francisco,

   CA: Chronicle Books.

In-text Citation:
Visage (2015)
(Visage, 2015).

2. Book, one author with only one name (like Cher).

Example:
RuPaul. (2010). *Workin' it!: RuPaul's guide to life, liberty, and*

   the pursuit of style. New York, NY: It Books.

In-text Citation:
RuPaul (2010)
(RuPaul, 2010).

3. Book, electronic version (like a Kindle book)

Example:
Lapin, N. (2015). *The rich bitch guide to love and money* [Kindle

Edition version]. Retrieved from Amazon.com.

In-text Citation:
Lapin (2015)
(Lapin, 2015).

4. Book with two authors

Example:
Simmons, N., & Byerly, J. C. (2016). *Keeping it real*. Columbus,

OH: Fake Shit.

In-text Citation:
Simmons and Byerly (2016)
(Simmons & Byerly, 2016).

5. Book with three or more authors

Example:
Beck, C. S., Chapman, S. A., Simmons, N., Tenzek, K., & Ruhl,

S. (2015). *Celebrity health narratives and the public*

health. Jefferson, NC: McFarland.

In-text Citation:
Beck, Chapman, Simmons, Tenzek, & Ruhl (2015) [1st time]
(Beck et al., 2015).

6. Book with an editor

Example:
Hannah, G. T. (Ed.). (2015). *The art of control: Developing your*

intelligent emotions and managing your life. Atlanta,

GA: The Ledlie Group.

In-text Citation:
Hannah (2015)
(Hannah, 2015).

7. Book with two editors

Example:
Williams-Davis, R., & Patterson-Masuka, A. (Eds.) (2015).

Intercultural communication for global engagement.

Dubuque, IA: Kendall Hunt.

In-text Citation:
Williams-Davis and Patterson-Masuka (2015)
(Williams-Davis & Patterson-Masuka, 2015).

8. Books with editions

Example:
Condon, J. C., & Masumoto, T. (2011). *With respect to the*

Japanese: Going to work in Japan (2nd ed.). Boston,

MA: Intercultural Press.

In-text Citation:
Condon & Masumoto (2011)
(Condon & Masumoto, 2011).

9. A chapter in a book

Example:
Simmons, N., Chen, Y.-W., & Kang, D. (2015). Emotions in

    race talk in the post-Obama era: Unpacking a dialogic

    pedagogy of talking back. In R. Williams-Davis & A.

    Patterson-Masuka (Eds.), *Intercultural communication*

    for global engagement (*pp. 275-287*). Dubuque, IA:

    Kendall Hunt.

In-text Citation:
Simmons, Chen, & Kang (2015)
(Simmons, Chen, & Kang, 2015).

10. A translation

Example:
Simmel, G. (1950). *The sociology of Georg Simmel.* (Kurt H.

    Wolff, Trans.). New York, NY: Free Press.

In-text Citation:
Simmel (1950)
(Simmel, 1950).

11. Book review

Example:
Simmons, N. (2016). Is this shit legit? [Review of the book *Bitch*

    slap APA, by N. Simmons & J. C. Byerly]. *XX*, 126-128.

In-text Citation:
Simmons (2016)
(Simmons, 2016).

12. Encyclopedia

Example:
Simmons, N. (in press). Naturalistic observation. In M. Allen

(Ed.), *The SAGE Encyclopedia of Communication*

Research Methods (pp. xxx-xxx). Thousand Oaks, CA:

Sage.

In-text Citation:
Simmons (in press)
(Simmons, in press).

13. Dictionary

Example:
bitch. (2016). In *Dictionary.com*. Retrieved from

http://www.dictionary.com/browse/bitch?s=t

In-text Citation:
bitch (2016)
(bitch, 2016).

Periodicals

Fucking Format: Periodicals are basically the shit that is published regularly (i.e., newspapers, newsletters, magazines, and journals).

Author, A. B. (year). Title of article. *Title of Periodical, xx,* pp-pp. doi:

- Always add the DOI if one exists.
- No DOI? Then use this fucking format: Retrieved from http://www.ican'tbelievethisshit.com
- Don't forget the volume number (xx) below, and if you have an issue number (See Chapter 5 & 9 for exceptions), put it in parenthesis after the volume number like this: *xx*(3), 543-589.

14. Article with one author

Example:
Simmons, N. (2014). Speaking like a queen in *RuPaul's Drag*

Race: Towards a speech code of American drag queens.

Sexuality & Culture, 18(3), 630-648.

doi:10.1007/s12119-013-9213-2

In-text Citation:
Simmons (2014)
(Simmons, 2014).

15. Article with two authors

Example:
Simmons, N., & Chen, Y.-W. (2014). Using six-word memoirs

to increase cultural identity awareness. *Communication*

Teacher, 28, 20-25. doi:10.1080/17404622.2013.839050

In-text Citation:
Simmons and Chen (2014)
(Simmons & Chen, 2014).

16. Article with three or more authors

Example:
Beck, C. S., Aubuchon, S., McKenna, T., Ruhl, S., & Simmons,

N. (2014). Blurring personal health and public priorities:

An analysis of celebrity health narratives in the public

sphere. *Health Communication, 29*(3), 244-256.

doi:10.1080/10410236.2012.741668

In-text Citation:
Beck, Aubuchon, McKenna, Ruhl, and Simmons (2014) [1st time]
(Beck, Aubuchon, McKenna, Ruhl, & Simmons, 2014).

17. Journal article without DOI (no DOI is available)

Example:
Simmons, N. (2012). The tales of *gaijin*: Health privacy

perspectives of foreign English teachers in Japan.

Kaleidoscope, 11, 17-38. Retrieved from

http://opensiuc.lib.siu.edu/cgi/viewcontent.cgi?article=1

087&context=kaleidoscope

In-text Citation:
Simmons (2012)
(Simmons, 2012).

18. Journal article, in press

Example:
Simmons, N. (in press). Cultural discourses of privacy:

Interrogating globalized workplace relationships in

Japan. *Journal of International & Intercultural*

Communication. doi:10.1080/17513057.2016.1142601

In-text Citation:
Simmons (in press)
(Simmons, in press).

19. Special issue journal article

Example:
Chen, Y.-W., Simmons, N., & Kang, D. (2015). "My family isn't

racist however…": Multiracial/Multicultural Obama-ism

as an ideological barrier to teaching intercultural

communication in a post-racial era. [Special Issue].

Journal of International & Intercultural

Communication, 8(2), 167-186.

doi:10.1080/17513057.2015.1025331

In-text Citation:
Chen, Simmons, & Kang (2015)
(Chen, Simmons, & Kang, 2015).

20. Magazine article

Example:
Byerly, J. C. (2016, May). Title of some shit: My shit don't

smell. *Healthy Shit, 23*(3), 126-128.

In-text Citation:
Byerly (2016)
(Byerly, 2016).

21. Online magazine article

Example:
Byerly, J. C. (2016, May). Title of some shit: My shit don't

smell. *Healthy Shit, 23*(3). Retrieved from

http://www.madeupcitation.com/getitgirl.htm

In-text Citation:
Byerly (2016)
(Byerly, 2016).

22. Newsletter article, no author

Example:
Fucking APA. (2007, January/February). *Bitch slap news @ a*

snap. Retrieved from

http://www.bitchslapit.net/gov/news/topstory.html

In-text Citation:
"Fucking APA" (2007)
("Fucking APA," 2007).

23. Newspaper Article with an author

Example:
Currie-Robson, C. (2014, January 22). Teachers tread water in

eikaiwa limbo. *The Japan Times.* Retrieved from

http://www.japantimes.co.jp/community/2014/01/22/gen

eral/teachers-tread-water-in-eikaiwa-

limbo/#.UxyVV4XskY2

In-text Citation:
Currie-Robson (2014)
(Currie-Robson, 2014).

24. Newspaper Article

Example:
Simmons, N. (2006, February 22). Using swear words to convey

meaning. *Fuck it Times,* pp. A1, A5.

In-text Citation:
Simmons (2006)
(Simmons, 2006).

25. Online newspaper article

Example:
Byerly, J. C. (2005, March 12). Bitch slapping APA. *The APA*

Times. Retrieved from http://www.apatimes.com

In-text Citation:
Byerly (2005)
(Byerly, 2005).

Unpublished & Informally Published Manuscripts or Works

Unpublished manuscripts are manuscripts that people were too lazy to publish. JK. This is shit that might be in progress, meaning it is in the fucking works, so chill! It might have been submitted to a journal, and some of those journals are as slow as molasses on a fucking cold night! This could also be work on a personal website – basically, nowhere real fucking formal, just a chill place to share yo' business.

Fucking Format:

Author, A. B. (Year). *Title of your shit.* Unpublished manuscript [or

"Manuscript submitted for publication," or "Manuscript in

preparation"].

26. Unpublished manuscript via a university

Example:
Simmons, N. (2003). *Bitch slapping this shit.* Unpublished

manuscript, Department of Communication, University

of Bull Shit, Columbus, OH.

In-text Citation:
Simmons (2003)
(Simmons, 2003).

27. Manuscript in progress or submitted for publication

Example:
Byerly, J. C. (2008). *Nursing goodies and APA shit: A*

theoretical perspective. Manuscript submitted for

publication.

In-text Citation:
Byerly (2008)
(Byerly, 2008).

- Don't tell where the damn thing has been submitted. There's this thing called "blind-review" and we wanna keep that shit confidential.
- Has your shit been accepted for publication, but isn't yet out? Treat it as you would an "in press" reference.

- Use this same fucking format for works in progress, but say "Manuscript in preparation" instead of "Manuscript submitted for publication."

28. Personal Communication

Example:
This should not be on your fucking reference list. APA says HELL NO, cite this shit in-text only.

In-text Citation:
(J. Byerly, personal communication, August 22, 2016).

29. Lecture Notes

Example:
Simmons, N. (2014). *Sexual health disclosure*. Personal

Collection of N. Simmons, Ohio University, Athens OH.

In-text Citation:
Simmons (2014)
(Simmons, 2014).

30. PowerPoint Slides

Example:
Simmons, N. (2015). *How to APA it like a champ* [PowerPoint

slides]. Retrieved from http://www.fakesitehere.com

In-text Citation:
Simmons (2015)
(Simmons, 2015).

Electronic Sources

Fucking Format:
Electronic sources are crazy as fuck. In fact, APA doesn't have one singular way to write out this shit. Therefore, please see each example below on how the hell to do it. Don't fucking freak out, it still follows the APA pattern of Author, Year, Title, and shit like that.

31. Internet article

Example:
JET Programme. (2013). *History*. Retrieved from

http://www.jetprogramme.org/e/introduction/history.htm

In-text Citation:
JET Programme (2013)
(JET Programme, 2013).

32. E-mail

Don't fucking put e-mails in your reference list. If someone asks you to do this, they don't fuckin' know APA. Give them a copy of this book and say, "Read this bitch!" Instead, e-mails should be cited as personal communications in-text.

(J. Byerly, personal communication, August 22, 2016).

33. Online discussion groups

Example:
Byerly, J. C. (2014, January 2). Re: Citing APA format

efficiently [Online forum comment]. Retrieved from

http://groups.apa.com/fake/url/loveit.html

In-text Citation:
Byerly (2014)
(Byerly, 2014).

34. Electronic mailing lists (AKA a listserv)

Example:
Simmons, N. (2000, October 31). Re: Bitch Slapping APA

[Electronic mailing list message]. Retrieved from

http://lists.bitchsla/making/this/up.htm

In-text Citation:
Simmons (2000)
(Simmons, 2000).

35. Blog Post

Example:
Simmons, N. (2015, August 14). Health privacy in Japan. [Web

log post]. Retrieved from

http://jetwit.com/wordpress/2015/08/14/jets-in-

academia-health-privacy-in-japan/

In-text Citation:
Simmons (2015)
(Simmons, 2015).

36. Blog Post Comment

Example:
J Byerly. (2016, August 22). Re: WTF is APA? [Web log

comment]. Retrieved from http://www.fakeurl.com/eatit

In-text Citation:
Byerly (2016)
(Byerly, 2016).

37. Vlogs (video-blog)

Example:
Byerly, J. C. (2015, March 2). Fucking APA fundamentals

[Video file]. Retrieved from

http://www.bitchslapit.com/yomama

In-text Citation:
Byerly (2015)
(Byerly, 2015).

38. Wikis

Example:
Cat. (n.d.). Retrieved November 19, 2016 from the Kitty Kat

Wiki: http://wikilicious.net/kitties/katzzz

Note: There is a retrieval date, only because the shit might change. Yes, this is a fucking exception to the rule.

In-text Citation:
Cat (n.d.)
(Cat, n.d.).

39. YouTube videos

Example:
[Bitch Slap APA]. (2013, May 5). Happy as fuck. [Video file].

Retrieved from http://youtube.com/aasdfasdfasdf

Note: Bitch Slap APA is the "screenname" or the "author" for the YouTube video. There may not be an official author, because they may not want you to know who they fucking are.

In-text Citation:
Bitch Slap APA (2013)
(Bitch Slap APA, 2013).

Technical & Research Reports

Fucking Format:
Author, A. B. (year). Title of work (Report No. xxx). Location: Publisher

- Is there a number (report number, contract number, monograph number, etc.)? Report that shit ASAP in parentheses immediately after the title (like in the above example).
- No report number? Then, leave that shit out.
- Did you retrieve the report online? Report it how you fucking found it: Retrieved from Agency name website: http://www.xxxxx

40. Corporate authored government report

Example:
U. S. Department of Bull Shit, National Institute of APA. (2002).

Managing bull shit: A guide to APA (NIA Publication

No. 234-23432). Retrieved from

http://www.nia.org.gov/seriously/wtf.htm.pdf

In-text Citation:
U. S. Department of Bull Shit (2002)
(U. S. Department of Bull Shit, 2002).

41. Corporate authored online task force report

Example:
America Association of Bull Shit, Task Force on APA. (2008).

Report of the AABS Task Force on the correct usage of

APA. Retrieved from

http://www.yougettheidea.com/pdf.htm

In-text Citation:
America Association of Bull Shit (2008)
(America Association of Bull Shit, 2008).

42. Authored report from nongovernmental organization

Example:
Byerly, J. C. (2005). *The contribution of bull shit to APA*

(Research Report No. 69.6). Retrieved from Research on

APA Alliance website:

http://www.are.you.seriously.com/making/me/typethissh

it.htm.pdf.lmnop

In-text Citation:
Byerly (2005)
(Byerly, 2005).

43. Issue brief

Example:
Employee Bull Shit Benefits. (1990, January). *Sources of APA*

health and other bull shit (Issue Brief No. 456).

Columbus, OH: Author.

• In addition to issue briefs, use this fucking format for working papers, corporate documents, and similar bull shit. Keep in mind the appropriate document numbers (if present).

In-text Citation:
Employee Bull Shit Benefits (1990)
(Employee Bull Shit Benefits, 1990).

Meetings & Symposium

Fucking Format: Use the following fucking format for unpublished symposia contributions, conference papers, and poster presentations. If such as published regularly, do this like you could a periodical. If what you want to cite is published in a book, use the book or book chapter fucking format.

Symposium:
Contributor, A. B. (year, month). Title of contribution. In A. B.

Chairperson (Chair), *Title of symposium*. Symposium

conducted at the meeting of Organization Name,

Location

Conference Paper or Poster Session:
Author, A. B. (Year, Month). *Title of paper or poster*. Paper or

poster session presented at the meeting of Organization

Name, Location

44. Symposium contribution

Example:

> Simmons, N. (2015, February). Privacy management and
>
> health issues. In M. Dainton (Chair), *Relational*
>
> *Research Symposium.* Symposium conducted at
>
> the meeting of the Relational Research
>
> Committee, La Salle University, Philadelphia,
>
> PA.

In-text Citation:
Simmons (2015)
(Simmons, 2015).

45. Conference paper

Example:
Simmons, N. (2015, November). *"I get diabetes just watching*

> *Paula Deen": Analyzing public responses to Paula*
>
> *Deen's type II diabetes diagnosis.* Paper presented at the
>
> One Hundred First National Communication Association
>
> Annual Convention, Las Vegas, NV.

- Get this shit online? Just add "Retrieved from" with the URL at the end after the location.

In-text Citation:
Simmons (2015)
(Simmons, 2015).

46. Conference paper abstract, retrieved online

Example:
Simmons, N., & Chen, Y.-W. (2014, November). *Just an*

imported "pinch-hitter": Ideological constructions of

foreign English language teachers in Japan. Paper

presented at the One Hundredth National

Communication Association Annual Convention,

Chicago, IL. Abstract retrieved from

https://www.natcom.org/uploadedFiles/Convention_and

_Events/Annual_Convention/100th_Annual_Convention

_2014/Saturday%20(10-7-14).pdf

In-text Citation:
Simmons and Chen (2014)
(Simmons & Chen, 2014).

47. Invited lectures or workshops

Example:
Simmons, N. (2012). *Honey, I have herpes: Sexual health*

disclosure. Presented to Dr. Gregory Janson's "Human

sexualities" undergraduate course, Ohio University,

Children and Family Services.

In-text Citation:
Simmons (2012)
(Simmons, 2012).

Doctoral Dissertations & Master's Theses

Fucking Format: Dissertations and theses are a lot of work and so you can find this shit in all sorts of places (i.e., personal websites, databases, etc.). Therefore, depending upon how you found it, will depend upon how you should cite it:

For a dissertation or thesis retrieved via a database:
Author, A. B. (year). *Title of dissertation or thesis* (Doctoral

   dissertation or master's thesis). Retrieved from Name of

   database. (Accession or Order No.).

For unpublished dissertations or theses, do this:
Author, A. B. (year). *Title of dissertation or thesis* (Unpublished

   doctoral dissertation or master's thesis). Name of Institution,

   Location.

48. Master's thesis

Example:
McKenna, T. (2010). *I'm retired? An examination of the*

   organizational and individual influences on adjustment

   into retirement and social identity as retired.

   (Unpublished master's thesis). Illinois State University,

   Normal, IL.

In-text Citation:
McKenna (2010)
(McKenna, 2010).

49. Doctoral dissertation, retrieved online

Example:
Simmons, N. (2014). *Negotiating boundaries in a globalized*

world: Communication privacy management between

foreign English teachers and Japanese co-workers in

Japan (Doctoral dissertation, Ohio University). Retrieved

from https://etd.ohiolink.edu/ap/10?0::NO:10:P10_

ACCESSION_NUM:ohiou1400259896

In-text Citation:
Simmons (2014)
(Simmons, 2014).

Audiovisual Media

Fucking Format: For a television or radio series, use the same fucking format as a book chapter, but list the writer and director in the author and editor positions. Just remember with all of this weird shit, the description of what it is goes in the fucking brackets.

For a movie or video, use the following fucking format:
Producer, A. B. (Producer), & Director, AB. (Director). (year). *Title*

of video [Motion picture]. Country of origin: Studio

For a music recording, us the following fucking format:
Writer, A. B. (Copyright year). Title of song [Recorded by A. B.

Artist if different from writer's name]. On *Title of album*

[Recording medium: CD, record, cassette, 8-track, etc.]

50. Episode from a television series

Example:
Byerly, J. C. (Writer), & Simmons, N. (Director). (2007). APA

like a bad ass [Television series episode]. In G. Funky

(Executive productive), *APA*. Columbus, OH: Byerly &

Simmons Broadcasting.

In-text Citation:
Byerly and Simmons (2007)
(Byerly & Simmons, 2007).

51. Video

Example:
Simmons, N. (Producer), & Byerly, J. C. (Director). (2017).

Responding to stupidity [Motion picture]. USA: Bitch

Slap Studios

In-text Citation:
Simmons & Byerly (2017)
(Simmons & Byerly, 2017).

52. Podcast

Example:
Simmons, N. (Producer). (2015, December 22). *Bitch slap APA*

[Audio podcast]. Retrieved from

http://www.bitchslapapa.org

In-text Citation:
Simmons (2015)
(Simmons, 2015).

53. Music recording

Example:
Byerly, J. C. (2008). Bitch slap APA. On *Fuck it* [CD]. New

York, NY: Simmons Records.

In-text Citation:
Byerly (2008)
(Byerly, 2008).

54. Map from the internet

Example:
Byerly County Geographic Services (Cartographer). (2011).

Population of dumbasses, 2000 U.S. Census

[Demographic map]. Retrieved from

http://www.i.cant.believe.this.shit.com/maps/demograph

ics.pdf

In-text Citation:
Byerly County Geographic Services (2011)
(Byerly County Geographic Services, 2011).

55. Photographs

Example:
Byerly, J. C. (Photographer). (2000, February 1). *Fugly*

[Photograph]. Columbus, OH: City Museum of Art

In-text Citation:
Byerly (2000)
(Byerly, 2000).

Court Decisions

Court decisions might have several dates. So, list all that shit out. Sometimes cases go a while, so listing only one date might make us think that shit only happened once.

> Fucking Format:
> Name v. Name, Volume Source Page (Court Date).

56. Case

> Example:
> Byerly v. Simmons, 245 F. Supp. 1199 (E.D. Wis. 1980).

> In-text Citation:
> *Byerly v. Simmons* (1980)
> (*Byerly v. Simmons*, 1980).

> • WTF is this example?! Let's break this shit down. This is a mock example of a federal district court for the Eastern District of Wisconsin in 1980. The volume number is 245. It appears in the *Federal Supplement* and starts on page 1199 of volume 245. Make sense? If not, you really should go back to fucking law school...

Legislative Materials

What do you do for testimonies and hearings? Following the fucking format below. Essentially, provide the title or number (there's probably some type of descriptive number) and the date like this:

> Fucking Format:
> *Title*, xxx Cong. (date).

57. Federal testimony

Example:

RU232: The APA ban and its effects on society: Hearings before

the Subcommittee on Regulation for Sanity of the House

Committee for Smaller Business, 121st Cong. 22 (1981)

(testimony of John C. Byerly).

- WTF? This fake testimony was supposedly given before a subcommittee of the U.S. House of Representatives during the 121st session of congress. It starts on page 22. In the fucking reference, make sure you have the entire title (as written in the official pamphlet, etc.), the subcommittee name (if any), and the committee name.

In-text Citation:

RU232: The APA Ban (1981)

(*RU 232: The APA Ban*, 1981).

58. Full federal hearing

Example:

America's need for APA format to strengthen the economy:

Hearing before the Subcommittee on Human Life of the

Committee on How to Life, House of Representatives,

103d Cong. 2 (2011).

- WTF? This fake federal hearing was held in 2011 during the 103d Congress in the U.S. House of Representatives. The hearing begins on page 2 of the hearing pamphlet.

In-text Citation:

America's need for APA (2011)

(*America's need for APA*, 2011).

8

ANNOTATED REFERENCES

Truth be told, the official APA manual doesn't say a fucking thing about how the hell to make an annotated reference list! Common speech is to call this an "annotated bibliography" – perhaps because it is easier to fucking say, but since APA calls the reference list "references" and not "works cited" or a "bibliography," as we already fucking discussed, we will refer to this as annotated references. Since APA doesn't give a fuck enough to mention how to throw this shit together, it is best to check with your higher power (i.e., professor, boss, pagan deity, or owner) on what the fuck they expect you to do. However, we do have some ideas on how to bitch slap this shit too.

Annotations are not fucking abstracts, conclusions, or introductions. Nor, should you be a lazy bitch and just cut and paste from your source into your annotation. That's called plagiarism asshole.

Annotations generally have a few sentences (sometimes 3-5) that summarize main points within the source. Ass-fucking annotations usually include an assessment of the quality of the fucking work related to your specific focus. For example, let's say you want to compose an annotated reference list regarding "privacy in cultures." In that instance, you should select research that aligns or speaks to your overarching topic. Within your annotation, after you summarize the shit outta it and such, you may evaluate its utility for your fucking work. Based off of APA's general fucking format, here is what we recommend.

Your annotated references should have two items, in this order:

1. Citation of your shitty source
2. Asshole annotation

Make sure that you double-space that shit and do NOT add a quadruple space between your reference citation and your annotation. This document should be double-spaced, just like the rest of your APA shit – don't fuck that shit up. You've been warned!

Don't forget your fucking title. You might title your annotated references as: (a) Annotated References, (b) the name of your theory or topic, or (c) whatever the hell your professor, boss, or owner said to do.

Here's a fucking example of how an annotated reference might appear:

Gecas, V., & Libby, R. (1976). Sexual behavior as symbolic interaction.

The Journal of Sex Research, 12(1), 33-49.

This article explores how one's sexual behavior is an expression of

one's symbolic environment, as well as how parents and friends

serve as influencing factors. They claimed that language is

instrumental to sexual arousal. The authors argued that sexual

behavior is overlooked in terms of study and, therefore, turned to

Burke and other scholars to explore how symbols are utilized during

sexual behaviors in order to create symbolic interaction.

*Notice that your paragraph is aligned with the hanging indent of your fucking reference. This isn't rocket science. Make that shit sparkle!

9

25 COMMON FUCK UPS

1. **Using a "magic" website to make your APA references.** Don't use a citation generator. They are almost always fucking wrong! Did you not read earlier when we said citation generators are the gateway drug to fucking up?! It's true! Sure, this can be a good starting point, but why not just make it from fucking scratch? Cakes are better from scratch, and so will be your APA reference list. It's more bad ass that way and then you don't forget to clean up all the shit that's wrong with it.

2. **Not knowing WTF your Reference page is called.** There are no "Works Cited" or "Bibliography" in APA. Instead, APA calls this "References." References should not be in bold when used as a title of your reference page. Double space this. Don't quadruple space after your write "References." That shit is annoying.

3. **Incorrect Reference Order.** Put your references in ABC order. Also, revisit Chapter 5. APA has a lot of rules on which shit goes first when. We sum that shit up there in lots of detail.

4. **Not putting two spaces after the period.** Except for your reference list, you should always put two damn spaces after your ending punctuation. Don't fuck that shit up. It's as easy as microwaving TV dinners…or popcorn.

5. **Improper Indenting.** Always indent your paragraphs except for the abstract.

6. **Forgetting to double-space.** Were you paying fucking attention? You must double-space in APA. None of that quadruple or single-spaced shit allowed!

7. **Font issues.** Use Times New Roman 12 point font unless otherwise indicated by your professor/employer.

8. **Comma use in Lists.** Use the oxford comma. Fancy bitches use the oxford comma, and APA is one fancy bitch. For instance, in a list of three or more items, use a fucking comma (i.e., apples, oranges, and bananas).

9. **Writing Numbers Out.** When writing numbers nine and lower should be spelled out; 10 and higher may be numerals. Related, if you start a sentence with a number, spell it out. (i.e., One vs. 1).

10. **Improper spacing.** Related to number six on this list: Do not quadruple space between paragraphs. Everything should be set to double-spacing. Leave it be! Don't hit "enter" twice. Also, check out the spacing mechanical bull shit rules in Chapter 4.

11. **Page numbers.** When doing in-text citations, it's "p." not "pg."

12. **Journal dois.** Add a doi. One probably exists if your article was published from 2000 to present. Look for it like you look for money in a couch cushion. It is there somewhere dammit!

13. **Periodical Issue Numbers.** Don't use an issue number for continuously paginated journals. WTF is pagination? That's when journals like to start every single damn issue on page one. Continuously paginated journals pick up where they left their shit off, even if that is page 1234.

14. **Block quote usage.** Block quotes should be used rarely and include 40 or more words. It is best to paraphrase and avoid block quotes all together unless you absolutely cannot paraphrase what is there (i.e., meaning that you gave a shit and tried fucking hard). Also, don't fucking forget that block quotes

do NOT have quotation marks and the punctuation is different from normal. The punctuation should come before the page number in parentheses, not after in this case. We know, it's weird as hell.

15. **Running head fuck ups.** The word "Running head" should only be on the title page. Look up some word processor tutorials if you can't figure out how to make the first page different from the rest of your pages. Also, "Running head" does NOT have a "S!" It is also NOT called a "Running header." Smfh...

16. **Corresponding References.** Make sure each in-text citation has a corresponding reference and vice-versa.

17. **Citing secondary sources, or sources within a source.** It is always best to go back to the original source, but if you do cite a secondary source remember to follow our advice in Chapter 6.

18. **et al. usage.** When using et al. for more than two authors in-text, don't forget you must list all authors' names the first time you cite them, unless you have more than six authors. You may only use et al. for the first in-text citation if you have more than six authors. Table 6.1 lists out this shit fucking beautifully for you.

19. **Hanging indents.** References must have hanging indents from the second line of each reference.

20. **Listing authors' credentials.** Don't list an author's degree such as a Ph.D. MA, etc. No one fucking cares.

21. **Acronym use.** Don't just use a fucking acronym. You gotta spell that shit out the first time and then tell us WTF it stands for in parentheses. So, the Center for Disease Control (CDC) is an example of how to fucking do it. Then, you may say, the CDC this, and the CDC that.

22. **Spelling/Years of References.** Make sure you spelled the fucking authors' names correctly in your references and in-text citations. That shit matters. Related, double-check the fucking years.

23. **Not using the correct edition of APA.** APA is now in the sixth edition. The fifth edition had some wacky shit. For example, if you are using retrieval dates in your references, you are using fucking fifth edition and fucking up in a major way.

24. **Incorrectly categorizing sources.** You need to know what you are fucking looking at. If you are looking at a magazine website, it is a fucking periodical. A newspaper online, is still a fucking newspaper online. It isn't just a damn "website." Ask a librarian or look that shit up, if you are confused on what type of source is what.

25. **Forgetting to fucking proof your work!**

10

SAMPLE PAPER

It helps to see a fucking sample. Now, we aren't going to give you a paper to steal and call your own, but we do have excerpts from a paper by Dr. Nathaniel Simmons that illustrates all this major bull shit we've been talking about (i.e., title pages, abstracts, levels of heading, and reference lists). You'll notice that the sample bounces around to showcase the most important APA portions of the paper. This also keeps the cost of this book down. The longer the fucking book, the more it costs.

About this paper:

This is a sample research proposal regarding the ethics of disclosing your sexual health status with sexual relational partners. In short, this is a conversation you should both be soliciting and giving freely, like so:

"Honey, I have herpes. Do you?"
"Thanks for telling me sex pot. No, I don't. Now, let's discuss how we can safely fuck."

Let's fight the fucking stigma about this shit and be grown-ass adults!

Sexually Transmitted Infections and Privacy Management:

Exploring Ethical Considerations amongst Sexual Partners' Sexual Health Status Disclosures

Nathaniel Simmons

Bitch Slap University

Abstract

This proposal seeks to understand ethical considerations of privacy management regarding sexually transmitted infection(s) (STI) disclosure. Utilizing Petronio's (2002) Communication Privacy Management theory, the author proposes a qualitative study utilizing focus groups and one on one interviews as a means to understand the ethics of disclosure of sexual health status. Participants will include college students from a large Midwestern university. Data will be analyzed via Lindlof and Taylor's (2002) thematic analysis and Glaser and Strauss' (1967) constant comparative method. Theoretical and practical implications will be considered.

Keywords: communication privacy management, ethics, sexually transmitted diseases, sexually transmitted infections, disclosure, privacy

Sexually Transmitted Infections and Privacy Management:

Exploring Ethical Considerations amongst Sexual Partners' Sexual Health Status Disclosures

On MTV's hit show, *The Real World* cast members must sign a waiver indicating that they don't have STDs, but at the same time must accept the fact that other people on the show might (Dodero, 2011). In fact, *The Real World's* contract states "If you contract AIDS or other sexually transmitted diseases while filming ["gonorrhea, herpes, syphilis, pelvic inflammatory disease (PID), Chlamydia, scabies (crabs), 'hepatitis, genital warts, and other communicable and sexually transmitted diseases or Pregnancy; etc."], MTV is not responsible" (Dodero, 2011). So if MTV isn't responsible, who is? Who might be responsible for the rest of society's "real world" sexual encounters? Is conversation and a condom our only methods of defense? If so, why aren't we having a sexual health status conversation with our sexual partners? The reality is, not having a sexual health status conversation could have negative consequences. Cunningham, Tschann, Gurvey, Fortenberry, and Ellen (2002) informed us that "Being reluctant to disclose such [sexual health status] information may strongly influence whether or not adolescents would be willing to get tested or seek care for sexually related diseases" (p. 334). However, we must keep in mind that adolescents are not the only one's having sex. What about the rest of us over the age of 18?

This study seeks to extend ethical questions raised by Ciccarone et. al (2003). Concluding their study of sex without disclosure of positive a HIV serostatus they posed the following questions: "Is it unethical to have sex without disclosing one's status when one's partner also does not disclose? Whose responsibility is it to disclose? Is the ethical obligation to disclose greater for the infected person" (Ciccarone et al., 2003, p. 95β). In addition, this paper seeks to explore ethical implications of soliciting one's partner's STI status.

RQ4: What role do ethics play as co-owners manage their partner(s) sexual health status?

RQ5: How do ethics influence the privacy management of sexual health status?

RQ6: How might STD/STI disclosure conversations enable and constrain sexual relationships?

RQ7: How might STD/STI information seeking conversations enable and constrain sexual relationships?

In order to gain insight into these research questions, and to extend the usefulness of CPM and explore its potential usefulness in this particular context, I propose the following methods.

Methods

Participants will be solicited from a large Midwestern university in the United States. Participants are chosen from this context due to accessibility to a student population and the belief that students will freely and openly discuss the topic with me due to my age (I'm not that much older than many college students) and the frequency of private disclosures past students and random people on the street have made to me. All participants must be 18 years or older at the time of the interview. Participants will be solicited via the following means of data collection.

Data Collection

With my research questions in mind and not knowing at the time what themes will emerge, I will advertise the research project in two ways: 1.) as one which seeks to understand sexual health status conversations and seeking individual interviews and 2.) seeking individuals to participate in a group discuss regarding sexual health status disclosure. A snowballing technique will be utilized at the end of each individual and focus group interview in order to receive recommendations and locate participants who might be willing to discuss the privacy management of their sexual health status. A snowballing technique should work well in this instance due to the potentially sensitive nature and private information related to this topic. In addition, I will contact the local university's Human Sexuality professor with hopes of soliciting participants. After gaining approval through my university institutional review board (IRB), I will begin the individual and focus group interview process.

Interviews. Upon consent, I will interview the participants in locations and times that are convenient for them. The interview guide will be composed of a series of open-ended questions that are designed to investigate ethical considerations regarding the privacy management of a positive STD/STI status. Additionally, questions will investigate an individual's ethical responsibility beliefs to solicit one's partner STD/STI status.

Interviews will range from 30 to 120 minutes and will be voice recorded. Upon completion, I will transcribe interviews via Dragon Speak, a voice recognition program. I will double-check each transcript; correcting and ensuring what was transcribed matched the original recording. This will ensure accuracy for data analysis purposes. In addition to interviews, I will record field notes during and after the interview sessions in which I will begin to note initial themes that seem to naturally emerge throughout the interviews.

Focus Groups. Lindlof and Taylor (2002) informed us that a "focus group can be a useful 'social laboratory' for studying the production of interpretations, perceptions, and personal experiences" (p. 182). This context will allow for a stimulation of ideas and expressed amongst its members (Lindlof & Taylor, 2002). My hope is that collecting data in multiple ways will strengthen my analysis by allotting for ample data with hopes of approaching saturation. In order to understand the complexity of STD/STI disclosure, multiple focus groups will be conducted. I will seek to create both complementary and argumentative interactions (Lindlof & Taylor, 2002). This will help me not only uncover sense making and theorizing in the

References

Afifi, T.D. (2003). 'Feeling caught' in stepfamilies: Managing boundary turbulence through
appropriate communication privacy rules. *Journal of Social and Personal Relationships,
20*, 729-756. doi:10.1177/0265407503206002

Afifi, T., & Steuber, K. (2009). The revelation risk model (RRM): Factors that predict the
revelation of secrets and the strategies used to reveal them. *Communication Monographs,
76*, 144-176. doi:10.1080/03637750902828412

Allman, J. (1998). Bearing the burden or baring the soul: Physicians' self disclosure and
boundary management regarding medical mistakes. *Health Communication, 10*, 175-197.
doi:10.1207/s15327027hc1002_4

Appiah, K. A. (2006). *Cosmopolitanism: Ethics in a world of strangers*. New York, NY: W. W.
Norton & Company.

Braithwaite, D.O. (1991). "Just how much did that wheelchair cost?": Management of privacy
boundaries by persons with disabilities. *Western Journal of Speech Communication, 55*,
254-274. doi:10.1080/10570319109374384

Bute, J. J. (2009). "Nobody thinks twice about asking:" Women with a fertility problem and
requests for information. *Health Communication, 24*, 752-763.
doi:10.1080/10410230903265920

Bute, J. J. & Vik, T. A. (2010). Privacy management as unfinished business: Shifting boundaries
in the context of infertility. *Communication Studies, 61*, 1-20.
doi:10.1080/10510970903405997

Charmaz, K. (2006). *Constructing grounded theory: A practical guide through qualitative
analysis*. Los Angeles, CA: Sage.

References

American Psychological Association. (2010). *Publication manual of the American Psychological Association* (6th ed.). Washington, D.C.: American Psychological Association.

ABOUT THE AUTHORS

Dr. Nathaniel Simmons is a communication professor. He first learned to bitch slap APA in an undergraduate APA course (hence the dedication). As a professional nerd, he researches privacy management (AKA how we keep secrets) in intercultural and health contexts. Dr. Simmons has published his research in (American) national, regional, as well as international journals. He co-authored the book *Celebrity Health Narratives and the Public Health.* Please see his website for his CV and more details: http://nathanielsimmonsphd.weebly.com/

John C. Byerly is a registered nurse and first learned how to bitch slap APA during his RN-BSN program. He is currently working on his Master's of Business Administration.

Nathaniel and John are married and live in the United States in Columbus, Ohio with their pug, Riblet.

49008300R00046

Made in the USA
Middletown, DE
02 October 2017